MARSHA RINEHART GRAHAM

Moments
in
Time

POETRY AND WRITINGS

To Carol,
You are so very special.
God Bless,
Marsha Graham

ISBN: 978-1-09831-304-3 (print)
ISBN: 978-1-09831-305-0 (eBook)

Forward

Can you remember times in your life that you'd like to say something but you just feel awkward or tongue-tied? Most people who know me would not say I was ever at a loss for words. Usually that is true, but when I'm emotionally involved, it is more difficult to say the right words at the right time.

Throughout my life I have written poetry for various occasions especially the ones that are emotional or special for me. Sometimes my poems are funny or at least I think they are. Others tell a story or share an event.

My basic talent is singing and I have sung since I could talk. I did a lot of solo work for weddings and churches. Most of my entertaining programs were done with my father and his singing buddies. We sang all over this part of Ohio. When my father became unable to do programs, I started working up interactive programs. These programs try to get the audience involved in singing, reminiscing and trivia. My bottom line is to have fun! Everyone says "the teacher comes out" during these events. I'm going to take that as a positive. Recently, I have been asked to speak at some events and those pieces are included in this book.

For the last several years I have written a Christmas poem that I share in my Christmas cards. It's my special gift (and thoughts) I want to share with those I care about. Now, I share them with you.

I started writing poetry at a very young age and it distresses me that I don't have some of my earlier work. Later on, I had the foresight to keep copies. In organizing this book, I surprised myself of important people and events that I did not write about. No offense was meant if someone feels left out. There are many lean years and I guess my energies were focused on my work at Marlington High School.

All the thoughts are original or stolen and my husband has made the most comments or corrections over the years. When I read my work to him, he adds his thoughts in word usage and sentence flow. Sometimes I agree - or not, and I thank him for his support, encouragement, and help.

Table of Contents

Autumn

God's paint has brushed the autumn leaves.
Fall colors whorl and float in the breeze.
This majestic beauty fills my spirit.
Can't you feel it? Can't you hear it?

I love to watch the geese honk by.
They make me smile and make me sigh.
"Dear God, Why is this time so brief?
Is it a prelude to winter's grief?"

"My child, I think you take this wrong.
Autumn time is to make things strong.
All things need to restore and rest.
Rebirth - is the part I love the best."

～～～

I love autumn and the changing colors. What a glorious
picture God paints for all of us to see! (Oct. 2004)

When I was in sixth grade, the song I sang for the Declamation
contest was called "God Painted a Picture". It was always one of
my mother's favorites.

Awesome Day

What an awesome day it is
This Monday, October twenty-seven
'Cause when I peeked out the window
I saw snowflakes whirling from heaven.

It's too early for this to happen
I'm not done frolicking in the leaves.
It can't be over. It's just too soon
As I watch the flakes swirl with the breeze.

I won't think of winter as cold and dead
It can be a time of warmth and light.
It isn't a season that I dread
Because I look forward to Christmas delights.

~~~~~

This was written October 27, 2008 as I was administering the
OGT (Ohio Graduation Test) at Marlington High School
cafeteria and gazed out the window.

Imagery

When I woke up this morning
The brisk wind whipped through the trees.
In its low pitch
It whistled a happy tune.

The soft yellow sun
Glimmered across the snow,
And the whole land
Reflected prisms like a mirror.

Little children were bundled
So they could barely walk
But, they were real excited
To see snowflakes piled knee-hi.

One small designed snowflake
Trickled from the sky
With its soft cooling effect
It hit me in the eye.

And then -
One small car
Came rumbling down the street.
Its heavy, black exhaust
Ruined the "perfect day".

Burma Shave Ditties

The air feels good.
You're out for a spin.
Buckle up for safety.
Speeders don't win.
Burma Shave

The road's a winding.
My top is down.
The sun's a shining.
I'll wear no frown.
Burma Shave

The air's refreshing.
The sun is high
I'll see you later.
I've got to fly.
Burma Shave

~~~~~~

AARTA (Alliance Area Retired Teachers Association) had a project to create Burma-Shave roadside poetry. The above were my contributions. Burma-Shave was a type of shaving cream and was famous for its unique advertising techniques of posting humorous four-lined poems along the road, one line at a time from 1925-1963. The last sign always gave their name – Burma-Shave.

Christmases Past

To reminisce of days gone by
It seems the years sure do fly.
This music box reminds me when
We were kids. Remember then?

All the presents we would shake,
And so at times we'd try to fake
Color, shape or a different size,
All to heighten our surprise.

One year Karen, the little sneak,
Opened presents and had a peak.
We knew what was in most every one.
Didn't that spoil some of the fun?

Every Christmas Eve we would make
A treat for Santa ~ maybe cake
We'd write him notes so he would know
Just where our gifts were supposed to go.

In our bedrooms we would pray
That we might hear Santa's sleigh.
Before we knew it, dawn had come
And boy, oh then, would we have fun.

In all my thoughts of Christmases past,
There's been one factor that will always last.
Our home was filled with songs and love,
And definitely blessed by God above.

~~~~~~

My oldest sister, Karen, swears she didn't peek but I think her
memory is going.

Christmas 2008

Nostalgia has really hit me
During this Christmas season.
I'm passing it on to you
So your packages have a reason.

As you open each of the presents
I hope that you will share
The story or memory behind the gift
Be it funny or sad; it's rare.

Some memories of our childhood
Is what I give to you.
So please relax and enjoy
And Yes, I Love You, too.

~~~~~

This poem accompanied a host of items that we had or used when we grew up. My husband made a wood golden-noodle-addle tree ornament. When we asked our mom what she got us for Christmas, she always said a golden- noodle-addle. I still have mine hanging on our tree. Some of the other gifts were Fizzes, wax-bottled sweet syrup, Jiffy popcorn, and a picture frame full of pictures and sayings.

I wrote the following lines in Shawn's (my husband) Christmas card in 2010. We had previously gone through some health issues and things turned around during this year.

We're so very lucky and have so many things.
It's been such a grand year.
I look forward to what the New Year brings.

It's like we have another chance during this stage in our life.
We're so very lucky and I'm glad that I'm your wife.

May this season strengthen us and fill us with His love.
Let's count our blessings one-by-one and thank the One above.

Memory Tree of Lights

I am honored to address you this afternoon for a couple of reasons: I love Christmas; this is a beautiful ceremony filled with love; I've been a hospice volunteer for 10 years; and 2 years ago lost my father and father-in-law in less than five months, maybe some of you knew them, Gordon Rinehart and Bob Graham. Both of them occupy a corner of my heart, so, I understand the bittersweet memories of celebrating Christmas without a loved one.

Now, since this program is called Memory Tree of Lights, I want to talk today about Christmas, good Memories and Christmas Lights. Christmas was and still is a wonderful celebration in our house and in our hearts. I love Christmas! I love decorations! I love giving presents! I like getting presents. I love doing something special to make someone smile! It takes me about a week to decorate the inside of our house. I know I'm slower than I used to be but I have really cut back in almost every area.

I like to decorate everything – that includes curtains, towels, soaps, little villages, and Santas galore. Now, I get the decorating part honestly because growing up, our house was decorated, from top to bottom – inside and out. It was like living in a wonderland. All the windows and mirrors were covered with glass-wax stenciled Christmas pictures. (I loved those simple decorations.)

My Dad outlined the house in lights and everything had to be perfect. He actually took strips of wood and drilled out holes that the lights went through so they would be perfectly straight. That's a little OCD for me. And, then, we'd hang wreaths in all the windows. Those were the red colored, heavy cellophane ones with a cardboard bow, and a candle light. Those are nostalgic memories.

I actually leave a Christmas thing up all year in most every room of our house – an ornament, a Christmas bear, a Santa fireplace matchbox. OK, the Thomas Kincaid Village is up because I'm too lazy to put it away every year. It's just easier to let it stay out. But, I do this so every time I look at it, it will remind me to be generous, to demonstrate God's love to all, and to soak up the positive power of hope.

One of my favorite things to do has always been going around and looking at Christmas lights. We did this as a family and my husband and I still do this. Let's reminisce for a second, especially if you've lived around Alliance:

- Thanksgiving Night - Lights down Main Street – wreaths, Santas, Reindeer

- East 62, after Homeworth Road and the train trestle, on the south side of the road- I don't know how many trees they decorated around that property.

- Reams Enchanted forest – that still continues

- Corner of old 62 and Morning Star-across from Molly Stark- That lasted for several years and then a neighbor complained about the traffic so it was stopped. So sad to see it end.

- Remember Across from Keiter's Crossing on Florence and Fernwood? Almost every house on both roads decorated. It wasn't necessary elaborate but most definitely cute and festive.

- Sebo's in Salem- that display is awesome

- Olgabay's Winter Festival of Lights in WV

- How about our own Silver Park? Love those lights.

- In Louisville, there are synchronized lights on Richards and then there are 3 houses off of Reno. Totally cool! The light show is synchronized to Christmas Music.

I'm sure you could add more and we (people) travel miles to look at the lights. Why is that? We came here today to watch the trees light up. There's just something magical and hopeful when the lights come on. Many ask what do decorations have to do with the true meaning of Christmas? WELL....

Every Christmas a write a poem called Christmas Thoughts and in 2009, my poem dealt with the Christmas decorations and the true meaning of Christmas. I'd like to share that poem with you.

I see the lights of Christmas as they twinkle in the night
And watch the peoples' faces gleaming with delight.
Do they understand their meaning? I ponder for a while.
They must grasp the meaning. I laugh, and then, just smile.
Maybe it would be easier to picture it like this:
Each light denotes a gift that Jesus gave to me.
Each star a reminder that He was meant to be.
Each wreath an unending circle just like His love for us.
Each Santa represents the good in all of us.
Each tree a declaration that He's our Majesty.
Colored all in red 'cause He died on Calvary.
Each bell a tinkling cymbal to announce the
Christmas season.
Each manger scene -it's obvious- Jesus is the reason.
So, as you look around at all the decorations,
Let your heart rejoice and make a proclamation -
Jesus will be the center of my Christmas season
Because I remember that Jesus is the reason!

Let's talk about the lights themselves. What kind of lights have you used on your Christmas tree? Some of you might have used real candles. That was dangerous. Most of us probably remember the medium sized or small Christmas lights. Then they came out with lights that look like a candle flame. I especially liked the frosted lights. Oh, and I do like bubble lights. I still use some of each type. When mini lights came out they were a big hit. Now we have rope lights, LED lights, dripping lights and who knows what they will come out with in the near future- Oh, yes, I just saw falling Rain lights. The whole point is - things change.

Change is inevitable. Doesn't mean it's for better or worse – just different. For most of us here, our Christmas celebration will be different this year because we've lost a loved one. For many of you this will be the first Christmas without someone you cherished. Be prepared. There will be some hard moments, some tearful moments, maybe anger or hurt all rolled into one and it weighs down your heart. Brace yourself, take a deep breath, and let it out slowly. Move past the pain and remember something wonderful about your loved one -- Their smile, their laugh, their favorite song, their favorite food, their favorite thing about Christmas. Remember something special and feel blessed that they were a part of your life.

When we're struggling with the loss of a loved one, it may be difficult to look at the fald-a-rall surround the Christmas season. People seem happy and carefree, music is playing, decorations, lights, parties, Christmas shopping. If the hoopla gives you problems, remember, those are outward signs of Christmas. Think of the true meaning of Christmas. In a few minutes we're going out in the lobby and light up the trees. The bulbs on the trees become a part of the Christmas décor for the hospital, and for you they represent the essence of a loved one. When the lights come on and reflect off the bulbs, let that dispersed light warm your spirit and give you hope.

I'd like to end with my Christmas Thoughts poem of 2017.

The clock on the mantel is ticking away
There are so many things to do and say
Christmas is coming; it's 'round the bend
Will our to-do list never end?

And yet, we look back on Christmases past
So many memories that need to last
We'll celebrate this year without Pa or Dad
Remembering sometimes makes us sad.

And yet, loving warmth fills our heart
Their spirits live ere we're apart.
Each new day a memory rises
It brings a tear, a laugh and surprises.

And yet, this special season brings to mind
Jesus gained two saints; each one of a kind.
They're singing in Heaven; we know it's true
'Cause they're having Christmas right beside You.

May the true spirit of Christmas shine through your grief and
give you hope.

~~~~~~

We lost Pa, Robert Paul Graham I, on Dec 28, 2016, which is
also the date of our anniversary. We lost my Dad, Gordon Dale
Rinehart, on May 3, 2017. This poem was difficult to
find balance.

Christmas Thoughts – 2000

Throughout the Year we celebrate
Various days of meaning,
Today we want to contemplate
What this season's bringing.

We hope that it brings joy to you
With heart-warming days
Of family, friends and others, too,
And fills your soul with praise.

We hope that it brings peace to those
Who need solace and rest.
So, throughout the New Year, we propose
They're at their very best.

When you recall the "Christmas Day"
And love fills your thought,
Then you can smile and gladly say,
That's what the season brought.

~~~~~~

I wrote this for our Administrative Christmas greeting to the Marlington High School staff from Rick Engle (principal), Duff Beamer (Assistant Principal), Keith Woods (Assistant Principal) and me (Dean of Students).

Christmas Thoughts – 2007

I'm so busy through the year
That I don't take the time
To Thank God for the blessing
That you are a friend of mine

Every card I send at Christmas
And every name upon my list
Has touched my heart in some way
I'm afraid of whom I missed.

Maybe it's been years ago
Or it happened just yesterday
But you, my friend, changed my life
In a big or significant way

So, "Thank you, God," for this friend
I'm sending this card to
That You may also touch their life
And bring their praise to You.

~~~~~~

So I started writing and inserting poems in my Christmas cards calling them Christmas Thoughts. I usually write them in late autumn. I choose a topic and after I mall it over, it just seems to come to me. Most poems take no more than 30 minutes to write, but it's a little gift/piece of myself to friends and relatives.

Christmas Thoughts - 2008

Christmastime is coming.
I can feel the excitement here.
For it's a very special time,
It's a shame it's once a year.

Just stop - and really think.
That statement is not true.
Christmas is not a yearly event;
It should last the whole year through.

So, open your eyes; rejoice
With gladness in your heart!
The Christmas Spirit is alive
And Christians need do their part.

Greet strangers with a smile.
And lend a helping hand.
Be thankful that you're able
And join our Christmas band.

Sing praises to the Lord!
Let your actions show His Love
And Christmas will come everyday
When we worship the One above.

Christmas Thoughts - 2009

I see the lights of Christmas as they twinkle in the night
And watch the people's faces gleaming with delight.
Do they understand their meaning? I ponder for a while.
They must grasp the meaning. I laugh, and then, just smile.

Maybe it would be easier to picture it like this:

Each light denotes a gift that Jesus gave to me.
Each star is a reminder that He was meant to be.
Each wreath an unending circle just like His love for us
Each Santa represents the good in all of us.
Each tree a declaration that He's our Majesty
Colored all in red 'cause He died on Calvary
Each bell a tinkling cymbal to announce the Christmas season
Each manger scene -it's obvious - Jesus is the reason.

So, as you look around at all the decorations,
Let your heart rejoice and make a proclamation -
Jesus will be the center of my Christmas season
Because I remember that Jesus is the reason!

Christmas Thoughts - 2010

Remember when you were just a kid
And Christmas was such a delight?
I didn't understand the significance of
What really happened that night.

For a kid it's all about Santa's gifts
And presents, treats or a toy,
But as I grew and learned the truth,
I comprehended the joy.

His love for us can overwhelm.
At times, it's hard to believe
That God's unconditional love
Is open for all to receive.

He gave us His Son in human form.
With this, man could relate.
We label this event - Christmas Day
And all Christians celebrate.

God knew His Son would come
Forever changing this earth;
And all because late one night
There was a Heavenly birth.

So during this Christmas season,
Look to the One above.
Thank Him for all His blessings.
Give Him all your love.

Christmas Thoughts - 2011

There's so much I want to say
But it's hard to get it out –
The joys of living everyday
And what this season's about.

The laughter, joy and Christmas cheer
It's bouncing through the air.
What a special time of year
In celebration of God's Heir!

Jesus wants you to tell His story
And bring joy to others, too.
Do it all in His name and glory
And that will glorify you.

Many do not know His love
Or feel His loving embrace,
But You were sent from above
To help our human race.

    Smile at someone. Say hello.
    Your spirit will be all aglow.
    Sing a song. Lift your voice.
    Make a difference. That's your choice.

After celebrating Mary's baby boy,
What's left within your heart?
Can you revive the Christmas joy?
Keep it spreading. That's your part.

~~~~~

May the joy of the Christmas spirit fill your heart with love!

MARSHA RINEHART GRAHAM

Christmas Thoughts - 2012

As you bustle through the store,
Stop and look around.
The season offers so much more
His blessings truly abound.

Jesus is definitely the reason.
We celebrate and worship, too.
Just ask throughout the season,
What would Jesus do?

Some people are happy-full of joy.
Others are serious, but kind.
Eyes light up when they spot a toy.
Memories come to mind.

He'd feed the hungry
Befriend the poor.
He'd help the crippled, too.
That's what Jesus wants
All of us to do.

Many are tired and weary.
Give them a listening ear.
Talk in a tone that's cheery.
Give hope that lasts the year.

He's the true Guiding Light.
His word will show the way.
Follow Him with all your might.
Take time, listen, and pray.

You make a difference; it's true.
It's right there in your heart.
Let His spirit fill you.
Reach out and do your part.

You are one of God's blessings.

~Merry Christmas

Christmas Thoughts - 2013

I know a little secret
It's nothing more than this.
The joy of the Christmas Spirit
Can truly bring you bliss.

It's not about the presents
That people give to you.
If that's what you're about
Then you don't have a clue.

It's all about the giving.
You must put others first.
It's not about the price tag.
That would be the worst.

The real joy of Christmas
Comes from deep inside
Use the Light of God's Gift
And let Jesus be your Guide.
Merry Christmas

Christmas Thoughts - 2014

Christmas time is almost here.
I long to see the lights and snow,
But, most of all I want to ponder
The Christmas of long, long ago

God sent to us His only Son,
The Babe ~ divine and true
I'm so thankful for His gift
And pray that you are too.

There's nothing wrong with celebrating
With presents, laughs and food
But, when I see a manger scene,
That truly sets my mood.

It helps me meditate on Baby Jesus
And all He means to me –
His life; His love; the blood He shed
Brings joy and sets me free.

So, as you observe this special season
Of happiness, joy, and love,
I hope you'll remember the precious gift
Of the Babe sent from Above.

Christmas Thoughts - 2015

What does it take to have peace?
Where can I get some relief?
If these are just two
Of the questions you spew,
Then you've missed the meaning of Christmas.

Our world is so full of doubt.
I wonder what that's all about.
Some lie to their brother
And fight with each other,
Then they've missed the meaning of Christmas.

Was there really a child that was born
In Bethlehem one starry morn?
The angels came down
The shepherds gathered 'round
Is this the meaning of Christmas?

God sent His Son from above
And sent His spirit through a dove
He gave us *The Light*
To ease our plight
And that's the true meaning of Christmas.

O come let us adore Him

He
was a
babe in
swaddling
clothes and yet,
he's so much more.
He lived so very long ago
but his age is evermore. His
Father gave Him as a gift to
Mary, Joseph and man. He is my
Savior and Confidant and that exactly was
His plan. Throughout His life He taught us;
the living Word He exemplified-so we would know
our God in Heaven and His name would be glorified. Who
was the babe in swaddling clothes whose impact was so
great, that after all these years we revere His name,
and He gives us reason to celebrate?
His
name
is Jesus

Christmas Thoughts - 2018

Bells chime out; it's Christmas time.
What a joyous time of year!
Love abounds and fills the air
Bringing everyone good cheer.

Yet there are some, I must confess
Whose hearts are dark and gray
For God is absent in their lives
A change for them – I pray.

Not everyone will accept
The gift that God has given
His Son who lived and died for us
And now is truly risen.

Without the birth of Jesus Christ –
The reason for the season,
It would only be another day
Not special for this reason...

He is The Light and Our Redeemer.
He fills our hearts with love.
We honor, adore and worship Him.
Christmas comes from the One Above.

And so, when you hear the bells ring out
To announce the Savior's birth
Lift up your eyes and rejoice
With Love and Peace on Earth.

Christmas Thoughts - 2019

The season is upon us.
It's very plain to see
With Santas, sleighs and reindeer
And lights on every tree.

These things evoke emotion.
It's Christmas time once more
And carols tell His story
To all – both rich and poor.

Open your heart and trust Him.
He gifts everlasting love.
You're life will be so much richer
When you talk to the One above.

It may be hard to give control
To the One you cannot see,
But He's the Christmas Baby Boy
Who died for you and me.

He's always right among us.
All you need to ever do,
Is bow your head and ask Him
And His peace will come to you.

So, stop and pray this Christmas season.
Ask Him to stand by your side.
He'll support, protect and love you
And be your eternal guide.

My Dad

MARSHA RINEHART GRAHAM

How I love a parade going by
With bands and floats under a big blue sky.
This year now, the best sight I'll see
Is my Dad, for the Parade Marshall he'll be.

He'll sit real tall with a great big smile
And wave to folks mile after mile.
He'll lead the parade in his jovial way.
Oh, won't it be such a very grand day?

The clowns and horses will do their thing
And people will cheer for the joy they bring.
And, my Dad will be the number one man
'Cause he's the finest in all the land.

~~~~~~

My Dad, Gordon Rinehart, was named Parade Marshall in 1995 for the Carnation City Festival's Grand Parade in Alliance, OH.

Spread the Word

Gordon's turning eighty-five
His health is good and he's alive.
He's not as quick as a flash
And we aren't having a **birthday** bash.

For Dad to hear, it's such a strain.
He uses his "ears", but it's a pain.
We'd like your help so mail him wishes
With birthday cards, hugs and kisses.

~~~~~

In 2010, we sent post cards and Dad received about 100
birthday cards.

MARSHA RINEHART GRAHAM

Why is Friday, August 14 a special day?
Gordon Rinehart was born that day.
He'll be 90. Isn't that grand?
So here is what we have planned.

An Open House from 2:00 'til 4
Don't knock. Just open the door.
Gordon lives at 2965 Ashwood.
Please stop by, wish you would.

He'd love to see you and celebrate
By having coffee and some cake
No gifts please – his request.
Just stop by and be our guest.

Can't make it? It may be hard.
Please consider sending a card.

Gordon Rinehart's Eulogy

How do you summarize a life of 91 years in a few minutes? You can't but I'd like to give you some thoughts and highlights.

Gordon was born to Erley and Effa Rinehart in 1925. Both of his parents taught in a one room school house although Grandpa was mostly a farmer. Education was valued and two of Dad's sisters taught school as well as Dad. He was their ninth child out of ten. And, yes, he did walk two miles along a hilly dirt road to catch a bus for the ten-mile ride to school and most years had perfect attendance.

One of Dad's tragic stories was at the age of three. Dad caught some sticks on fire in an open fireplace, ran into a wardrobe which caught some clothes on fire and started the house blazing. The result was total destruction of the house and practically all of the furniture.

When Dad was in third grade, his teacher disregarded the fact that he had the highest grades in the class and perfect attendance. He was the only one not promoted. So, he repeated the third grade with the highest grades and perfect attendance **again**. That would never happen in today's world.

In one of Dad's favorite songs: (sing) There's a place dear to me where I'm longin' to be with my friends at the old country church. That is Job's Temple where he attended church. It still exists and yes, it is on the side of a mountain.

During his senior year at Normantown, he was President of the Student Council and of his class. In January 1943, a ruling was issued stating that anyone who had three and one half years of high school credit and who would not be eighteen before the end of the term would qualify to go to college for the remainder of the year. (I guess that was 1943's version of post secondary classes.) The catch was that you would enter the service after graduation. Dad graduated in May and was salutatorian, but the thing that hurt his pride the most was that the one who had better grades was a girl. (I guess that's why God blessed him three daughters.)

He joined the Navy and was in the 117th battalion of the Seabees. He spent most of his time in the Pacific. On a 30 day leave, his sister Gwen went home to see him and she brought her friend. That's how he met our Mother, Dorothy Mundy. After he was discharged they married in Sept. of 1946. They lived in Canton, OH where Dad worked for The Timken Roller Bearing Company and Karen Kay was born.

In 1948, they moved back to Glenville, WV so Dad could complete his college degree. His first teaching job was in Ravenswood, WV where Linda Lee was born.

In 1952, his teaching brought him to Alliance, Oh and I was born that year. Years roll by and Dad is very active in the school and community. He received many awards and honors and those are listed in his obituary but he was especially honored to be a 33 degree Mason and devoted many hours to the Masonic order.

I asked my sisters what their most prominent memories of Dad were. Karen's first comment was that Dad and she had the mumps together. In WV on Spruce Run about 50 yards off the front porch, there was a metal target for shooting practice where Dad taught Karen to shoot. Karen particularly remembers the day Dad was target practicing, the bullet ricocheted and skimmed Dad across the temple.

Linda's memory was of Dad driving a car load of middle school cheerleaders to the games. Most parents were still working until five but with Dad being a teacher, he was available to transport a bunch of exuberant girls. She followed up with, "I don't know how he tolerated us." Linda also remembers Dad coming home and if he was stressed out he picked up his guitar and sang his troubles away.

I had a kaleidoscope of images of us singing together through the years. If anyone paid us for singing, he gave the money to charity. He told me music was a gift to be given away. Dad thought he was a jack-of-all-trades. He would attempt most anything and usually succeeded. As a carpenter, he finished off the garage and downstairs. As a gardener and landscaper, he planted loads of flowers and some vegetables. He was always an orator and a musician. He thought he was an electrician and one year he wired a load speaker in the back hallway by our bedrooms so he could crank up the radio and wake us up. Then, he would look at us so innocently and say, "I never said a word."

Teaching was not the highest paying job and Dad had a variety of secondary jobs: When he wasn't furthering his education in summer school, he taught summer school; he worked the front desk at the YMCA; He was a part time chemist at B & W Research; He also critiqued Science textbooks for Holt, Rinehart & Winston Textbook Publishing Company. (Unfortunately, no relation)

I found his birthday card from 1977 from his Mother. Grandma wrote:"... I remember you once said, 'My ultimate aim in life is to be a respected citizen in the community where I live.' I believe you have accomplished that and more."

At a relatively young age, we lost Mom to cancer and Dad married Helen Cope France. They had ten happy years together – traveling, laughing and making the world around them a more positive place. Sadly, God called Helen home.

In 1994, he met and married Mary Jane Haddad. Until the last few years, they shared their time between Florida and Alliance and cultivated numerous friendships, hosted several dinner parties, and praised the Lord for all His blessings.

Dad was noted for his little quips about life such as: It's a good day to be alive or it's a great life if you don't weaken. If someone asked him how he was doing? Dad would respond, "If I was any better, I'd need a doctor."

For his 80th birthday we asked people to write their memories of Dad and compiled them in a notebook. Many of you here were a part of that project and bless you because he has read those repeatedly and relived many memories. I'd like to share some of those comments which give a snapshot of his character and personality:

- Harold Hall, former superintendent of Marlington Schools wrote: Gordon could always bring extra life to a gathering of friends with his humorous stories and love of music. He will always be the "good humor Man" to me.

- Ede Carretta, retired teacher, said: One of the best in-service speakers ever was Gordon himself. The most memorable line was: Are we doing things TO kids or are we doing things FOR kids?

- But what I remember most of all is your smile, your positive outlook, your integrity, your support and your enjoyment of everyday, says Wendy Williams, retired teacher.

- Alan Andreani wrote, I feel fortunate to have known you as a teacher and as a friend. James Truslow Adams said, "There are obviously two educators. One should teach us how to make a living and the other how to live." You are one of those extremely rare people that can teach both.

- Nancy Schwan called him "the most positive person on the planet". She gave count of one day when she came to school all upset because she had a flat tire. In your unfailing optimism and infinite wisdom, you said, "That's okay, Nancy. Only one tire is flat; the other three are nice and round, aren't they?"

- Mary Jo Stertzbach wrote; "I didn't realize when Marsha became my best friend that I was getting a great second family as well. I was always so proud to tell everyone that you were my Adopted Dad. You inspired me with your positive attitude and your love of learning. You brightened my life with your love of music and laughter. You cared for me with your love and generosity.

- Diana Teeters stated: Our teacher – our neighbor. We weren't sure about living next door to our old teacher, that very "Straight Laced Teacher". Were we in for a surprise! Who else would shoot a pheasant out of their bathroom window!! Wake our children with cannon shots and host pool parties. We spent hours trying to keep our property up to Gordon's standards. He said he always did that for us."

- It is abundantly clear that your family tree has three daughters who have incomprehensible love for you. Nonetheless, our bond is no less transparent to us as you have been for quite some time and continue to be a father figure to me, signed your son, Albert Admonius.

- Lee and Bev Grable wrote that Valentine's Day took on new meaning with the parties hosted by Mary Jane and Gordon.

- Paul Chapple, a Masonic friend, wrote: Just recently I read some words that apply to you, my friend. The best sermons are lived, not preached.

I'd like to finish with a poem I wrote to Dad for Father's Day in 1981:

> I often write poems about people I know
> And this one is of no exception,
> For it's of a man I dearly love,
> A man of mortal perfection.
>
> Now you may say this is impossible.
> Some even say I'm mad.
> But here's my response to all of this,
> "Then you haven't met my Dad."
>
> His mankind service is not worldwide.
> He works mostly within our state;
> And there hasn't been one man I've met
> Who hasn't said, "He's great!"
>
> No matter what the occasion is
> To greet someone or to part,
> He always has a song on his lips

And the melody fills his heart.

Now, he has taught me right from wrong.
As a role model he's superior.
For when I compare him to other dads.
They all seem so inferior.

So for the courage he's given to me
to achieve to be on top,
I'd like to say, "I Love you, Dad,
And so thankful you're my Pop."

I hope everyone here feels their life is richer for having known our Dad.

MARSHA RINEHART GRAHAM

Easter

May we remember the One above
Who gave us His son to love.
But it wasn't a loss,
Jesus carried the cross.

Our sins were barred by Jesus
Whom God put on earth to lead us
He showed us the way
But for this He did pay.

When He died it was hell
But Christians know very well
From the grave He arose –
Just as God chose.

It's fitting at this time of year
When people are of good cheer,
That we worship the grave
And the life that He gave.

In addition to our body's rebirth,
May we look to the new budding earth,
For life is anew
Just as God knew.

May our souls be like the flowers
That grow stronger in spring showers,
For the Reign of Him
Saved us from sin.

Father's Day

MARSHA RINEHART GRAHAM

Today I'll take the time
To say that you are mine
On Father's Day I will say
Dad, you're great; you're fine.

Some Dads are pretty weird-
Tall, fat and with a beard
But my Dad's short and thin
And has a double chin.

Some Dads scream and shout
And make their daughters pout
But my Dad he's not cruel
He just makes me go to school.

Some Dads really stink
They don't even try to think
But my Dad, he's a brain
And sometimes a little *pain.*

You're tops on the list
And here's a big kiss
From the person who made you
What you are today
    A DAD!

~~~~~~

I found this poem when cleaning out my Dad's papers. My best
guess is early 1960's when I was around 10. It's a handmade
card of folded pages, punched out with ribbon, hand-drawn
pictures, and pasted pictures from magazines.

I often write poems about people I know
And this one is of no exception,
For it's of a man I dearly love,
A man of mortal perfection

Now you may say this is impossible.
Some even say I'm mad.
But here's my response to all of this,
"Then you haven't met my Dad."

His mankind service is not worldwide.
He works mostly within our state;
And there hasn't been one man I've met
Who hasn't said, "He's great!"

No matter what the occasion is
To greet someone or to part,
He always has a song on his lips
And the melody fills his heart.

Now, he has taught me right from wrong.
As a role model he's superior.
For when I compare him to other dads,
They all seem so inferior.

So for the courage he's given to me
To achieve to be on top,
I'd like to say, "I Love you, Dad,
And so thankful you're my Pop."

～～～

Gave this poem to my Dad for Father's Day in 1981 and read it
to close his eulogy on May 8, 2017.

Father's Day 1987

A Father's love is special
It's plain enough to see
How much he loves
How much he does
For all his family.
This love we have together
Is rather hard to measure
But on today
I want to say –
You're the Dad I treasure.
I feel that I'm quite lucky
In many ways that's true
'Cause you're the Best
You beat the rest.
Dad, know that I Love You!

~~~~~

I gave this to both my Dad, Gordon Rinehart, and to my Father-in-law, Robert (Bob) Paul Graham I. Both of these men were wonderful role models and fun to be around.

We've done a role reversal
In the last few years, it's true.
I don't mind and wander why?
It's 'cause I so love you.

You were my first love, Daddy
And I followed you around.
I went into teaching and singing
'Cause that's where our talents abound.

Even if you do not know it
And there are days it could be clear
I hope you always *feel* it
That I love you, Daddy Dear.

So on this special day in June
When Fathers should have their way
I wish for you peace, love and joy
And a Happy Father's Day.

                    Love

~~~~~

June 19, 2016 is the last Father's Day my Dad celebrated.

A Mother's Love

My mother is a part of me.
She gave me life from her body.
She fed me; took care of me,
Taught me right from wrong
And when I was very small,
I slumbered in her song.

During the pains of childhood
She kissed away my tears,
And all those loving memories
Stay with me through the years.

The spirit from her soul
Filled our home with love
I know that I've been blessed
By the wondrous One above.

For God gave me a dear Mother
Whose heart is of pure gold.
For every ounce of love in the world,
She's returned to me ten-fold.

So, I hope that I can bring her joy
On this eleventh day of May
By saying that I love you -
And Happy Mother's Day.

~~~~~

The year is 1980 and my Mother who turned 54 less than a month ago had been fighting cancer for a little over two years. This was a very difficult time. This poem was read at her funeral by the minister.

MARSHA RINEHART GRAHAM

Mother's Day

~~~~~~~~~~~~~~~~~~~~~~~~~~~~~~~~~~~

No matter what I do or say
Mere words cannot express,
The richest love I have for you
So deep within my breast.

For who can say how great you are
I know that I cannot,
And yet I want to tell you
You reign so far on top.

You're always in my thoughts and prayers.
You're with me night and day.
And when I need a helping hand,
I think of what you'd say.

And even though someday we'll part
I know now I'm not afraid,
For you will be right by my side
That I may follow the path you've laid.

No matter how soon that day may come,
No matter what day it may be,
We'll share the love that we have now –
The love between You and Me.

~~~~~

Mom was dying of cancer when I wrote this poem and she died
June 26, 1982.

The talk you hear 'bout Mothers-in-law
I know sometime is true.
But lucky me - I'm the exception.
To have One as Great as You.

Your shoulders are strong; your heart is open -
Your love and warmth are felt.
When God shuffled the mother-in-law cards,
The ace of hearts I was dealt.

Now, when I say, "I love you",
I say it with no fear,
For I am proud to have you,
Someone so thoughtful and dear.

So, on this wonderful tenth of May
In the year of eighty one,
I'd like to say, "I Love You, Mom
For all the things you've done."

Happy Mother's Day '81

~~~~~

My mother-in-law, Dorothy Marie Graham, was a warm, wonderful and caring person.

Mothers are something special.
There's so much truth to this.
Be it the healing from their hands
Or the warmth in their kiss.

The special love they give you
Enriches your soul and mind.
That's why this special type of love
Is so difficult to find.

Some people wish they had it.
Some people never will.
That's why a mother's role
Is so very hard to fill.

~~~~~

Written for Dorothy Graham for Mother's Day in 1983

MARSHA RINEHART GRAHAM

Happy Mother's Day
May 10, 1987

Although you aren't my Mother
And you'll never take her place,
I want to say, "I love you"
And love your warm embrace.

You fill my heart with gladness.
You give comfort and caress.
It helps fill the emptiness
So deep within my breast.

So, on this blessed Mother's Day
I hope that I can do
Some small little thing to show
How much that I love you.

~~~~~

I wrote this for my Mother-in-law and Helen Francis Rinehart,
my step-mother. Both were very lovely ladies who gave
unconditional love.

A Mother's love is enduring
Through childhood and through time.
A Mother's love is endearing.
A Mother's love is divine.

So on this, Your Special Day,
We want that you should know,
And we just have to say
That we both love You so.

~~~~~

Written inside a card for Dorothy Graham on
Mother's Day in 1991

We all know it's Mother's Day
And you wouldn't want a fuss,
But a special time is set aside
To express love from both of us.

Even though our love's always present
Every minute all year through,
Today's the day, Dear Mother,
To say that we love You.

~~~~~

Written inside a Mother's Day card for Mom Graham
May 12, 2002

Saying Good-bye

To Lois Shimp, our church organist, 1991

Every time I go to tell you
How much I'll miss you so,
I cannot find the right words
And tears begin to flow.

So I'm writing them on paper
These words I can't express.
"I'll sorely miss you, Lois,
From deep within my breast."

You've been my teacher and my friend
For at least the past twelve years
That's why it's hard to say, "good-bye"
And brings my eyes to tears.

You've filled our church with music.
It swells within my heart.
Which makes it so much harder
That you must have to part.

I wish for you life's beauty.
Your happiness is a must.
I'll patiently wait until God
Returns you home to us.

~~~~~

Lois Shimp was the organist at Science Hill church for many years. Our choir did not perform at the early church service so Lois played and I sang for many Sundays. Lois' husband was transferred down south and she had to move.

At Death's Door

Today I sit and watch her sleep.
Breathing's shallow; she's bundled up.
My heart lurches; it wants to weep
For this frail lady whose time is up.

From time to time, she opens an eye
And looks at me unknowingly
I ponder life and then I sigh
Praying to God full knowingly.

He's the only One who can save her
And comfort her in His arms.
Oh, wait a minute. I felt her stir
Or is she just rocking in God's arms?

I'm not sure how many will miss her
In current friendships she's rather poor.
But, when she knocks and He answers,
God will open Heaven's door.

~~~~~~

I am a Hospice volunteer and this was written at the bedside of one of my patients on October 29, 2010.

Crossing Over

When I knocked at death's door and Jesus answered,
I felt He had plans for me.
I walked into Heaven's white brightness
And I knew at last I was free.

I felt no pain or trembling
And it seemed I was floating on air.
I grinned as I looked all around me
Because most of my family were there.

As I looked back over my shoulder,
You were crying and it wrenched my heart.
I tried to reach out to reassure you
But my hand couldn't grasp any part.

I've left for now but don't be sad
For you were my angel on earth.
Rejoice! Be glad! I'm in His care
And that means more than I'm worth.

Remember God's love with a song in your heart.
Be cheerful and help others along
That they may know God's peaceful Heaven
And join in singing His song.

~~~~~

This poem was written on Palm Sunday, April 17, 2011.
April 17 would have also been my Mother's birthday.

Sisters

Forty-five years ago
A little babe was born
In Ravenswood, West 'Ginny
Early one frosty morn.

Some say it was a hospital.
Others say that it was not.
It really makes no difference
For this special tiny tot.

In 1950 that very year
A Northeasterner blew true,
And Linda Lee, the little babe,
Nearly froze and did turn blue.

That was just the start of things
To come this baby's way,
And October Twentieth still is
A very special day!

Throughout these pages
We hope you will see
That "This is your Life"
Our sister Linda Lee.

~~~~~

For my sister Linda's 45th birthday, Karen, my other sister, and I put together a picture album. Karen had gotten all the old slides from Dad and she took pictures with her new camera from the projector screen. Karen and I had a great time laughing at all the funny pictures-especially the ones of Linda. (1995)

Many people we take for granted
And though this shouldn't be -
Not to tell you how I feel
Would be quite negligent of me.

Though it's often left unsaid,
Mere words cannot express
The admiration I have for you
So deep within my breast.

When my body and mind are troubled
And you're not physically near,
Just knowing you're a thought away
Helps sustain me, Sister Dear.

I know I don't usually tell you
'Cause we're so often apart,
But my love for you, Dear Sister
Is embedded in my heart.

O.K. it's a little sappy but I think I must have been missing the sisterly contact. I gave this poem to both of my sisters for their Oct. birthday in 2004. *(Linda Stout (left) and Karen Rinehart-my sisters.)*

Work in progress

Karen and Linda's Birthday 2008

Our lives have varied from the start
But there has always been a link
It's been years since we left home.
Time flutters like a blink.

Our times together have always been
Precious moments so rare.
I know it's hard to find the time
So I treasure them with care.

Through the years as our lives change
If you need a listening ear
Please remember I'm a call away
And will always be here.
I'll always be there, never fear.

~~~~~~

I wrote this on July 22, 2008 waiting for Linda Johns Schillig
to get her hair done. It's maybe for Linda and Karen for their
birthday to put in the purse frame but I'm having heart
problems this week so the last stanza might not be true. As it
turned out, I made a collage for the picture frame of childhood
products, sayings, places, and movie stars.

The Ladies of Magnolia Street

This past September I had a unique experience that I would like to share. My sister, Linda had a bilateral mastectomy and because I retired in June, I had the opportunity to fly to Florida and be with her and her family through the first part of this crisis. She's doing well and started her chemotherapy at the beginning of October. But, the story I want to tell is about her friends and neighbors.

About a week after Linda received the news and could talk about her breast cancer without crying, the Ladies of Magnolia Street threw her a block party. As she entered Andrea's house, there was a receiving line of 12 Magnolia Ladies waiting for Linda with hugs and tears. This gave Linda the opportunity to confront and to explain to all of them at one time. Luckily, after the initial release of panic, anxiety and grief, the atmosphere turned festive with lots to eat and plenty to drink. There was a basketful of gifts so it seemed more like a shower. And in fact, it was. It was a showering of love and comfort. Linda opened gifts from "In the Pink": slippers, soap, arm comfort pads, skin softeners to use during chemo and camisoles. ("In the Pink" is a local store that caters to the needs of breast cancer patients.) Unfortunately, this occasion happened before I arrived and I missed this outpouring of love and support.

From the onset of this adventure, Susan D. has been Linda's eyes, ears, comforter and sounding board. She has gone to every doctor appointment and taken copious notes. What a devoted friend and a superb idea! In dealing with a surgeon, a radiologist, an oncologist, a neurovascular plastic surgeon and an anesthesiologist, everything started to jumble together. In addition to providing a chronological account of events, Susan's reference book helped review opinions, lead discussions and write questions for the next visit.

Within one hour of arriving at my sister's house from the airport, Susan D. came over to meet me holding out a hello gift of designer chocolate. O.K. I figured this woman truly understood the need for comfort food. She was delightful and a rock through my whole visit. Two hours later, Pam S. arrived and told Linda, "I came to meet your sister." Because I don't live in an area where the neighbors are within whispering distance, I was taken aback at the friendliness of these people.

The next day was Linda's surgery. Susan D. showed up with a picnic satchel full of sandwiches, drinks and munchies. She said, "We're going to be here a long time." We staked out an area of the waiting room and had an all day marathon. Linda had to be at the hospital at 10:00a.m. and she returned from the recovery room at 8:30 p.m. Who would have thought about bringing food? Susan did ~ for all of us.

The day after surgery several girls from Magnolia Street showed up to check on Linda. Andrea, Debbie, Pam and Susan are delightful, funny, caring and LOUD. I'm surprised we did not get kicked out, but these women are amazingly supportive of each other. Linda R. actually made my sister an adorable breast cancer survivor lap quilt. Many of the neighbors sent flowers, cards, gifts and food and have continued doing so.

Pam S. lived four houses down and had a pool which I used most every day while Linda took a nap. Susan D. invited me to supper and lunch on various days. It felt like I knew these women for years and that we were kindred spirits. We talked for hours and shared our thoughts and dreams. They invited me to their book club meeting where I met even more ladies from Magnolia Street.

It was good to see how supportive Linda's husband, Lans, was, as well as my niece Katie, and my nephews, Max and Zac. I have regretted not getting to spend much time with them over the past years. This situation has helped bridge the distance. What was even more assuring was that Linda had people within yelling distance who aren't afraid to be pushy when necessary. (We're all guilty about not asking for help when we need it.)

One day on the way home, Linda and I stopped at the local exquisite gift store. Linda was running out of energy so she stayed in the car and I went in for a look. I started talking to the owner, Carol, and I told her how several things looked familiar. When I related who I was, Carol left her store and went to the car to see Linda. I was flabbergasted that a shop owner would do that. Carol doesn't live on Magnolia, but she's Pam's best friend which makes her extended family.

A few days before I left, Susan D. had ten people over for a seafood low country broil dinner to celebrate Linda's speedy recovery and neighborhood camaraderie. It was magnificent! On my last night, Pam S. brought me a gift to mark my adventures on Magnolia Street. I received several pleas to come back soon and to think about moving to Florida. I never knew how close a neighborhood could be and hope that Magnolia Street is not the only street where the people make a difference.

~~~~~

This article was published in our local paper,
"The Alliance Review", on Tuesday, October 13, 2009
for breast cancer awareness.

Special Events

I am a member of Delta Kappa Gamma, Gamma Alpha Chapter.
This is an organization for female educators. As vice-president,
I joined our chapter president, Linda Hempstead, at the state
convention. I have a hard time sitting still so I write my report
for our chapter members.

As I walk into this draped Pavilion
In the corner the sun streams in.
It draws my attention
So I sit in its warmth.

I wonder if this is a true building.
The wall at my back is white plastic.
I can feel the cool air seeping through
But it does have clear windows.

We must be close to a major highway,
Because traffic noise provides background music.
The protocol of the meeting
Is followed to a tee.

The state officers sit at a raised platform
As chapter Presidents sit facing the head table.
The extras (that's me) are sitting at round tables in the back
While chandeliers hang from the draped, dropped ceiling.

The committee chairs all line up
The various reports are given
Some ruffle feathers and others soothe
But everyone is trying to be efficient.

Do these people take a break?
I'm having a hard time sitting still

I'm not sure I know exactly what's going on,
But I'm sure I'll learn as time goes on.

People constantly come and go
It's hard to make a count
So far, I think it's 122
But that would be give or take a few.

What are the goals of this whole group?
To help promote and support female educators
To encourage and aid girls in Afghanistan
To spread the news and grab the "gold key"

Ohio Historical Center has a bunch of our stuff
That documents the Alpha Delta State.
It's been cleaned up and reorganized
And we have a reader-friendly state history of 70 years.

A project fund has been established
To plan and celebrate our 75th year
In 2013 this milestone will happen
So let's all plan and join the cheer.

Everyone has their own little goal.
Today puts it all together.
So Alpha Delta State we are here
To gather information for the year.

~~~~~

Written on November 3, 2008 at the Alpha Delta State
Convention at the Crowne Hotel in Columbus, OH

Independence Day 2008

Come let us celebrate
Our Independence Day!
Give thanks to God and all our troops
For with their lives they did pay.

They paid for our freedom
Of religion and of speech
Give thanks to God and all our troops
Especially those within our reach

With my head held high
As our flag rolls by
And it flutters in the breeze -
My eyes fill with tears
For it vanquishes my fears
And all I said was - please.

Please God, protect all our troops.
Keep them warm and safe.
They're fighting for my freedom
So I may live in a better place.

Come let us celebrate
On this - the Fourth of July!
Give thanks to God and all our troops
For on them we rely.

National Honor Society

I was asked to be the guest speaker at Marlington High School's National Honor Society's Induction in March 2019. Their two advisors, Mr. Chris Locke and Mr. Jeff Oyster, were former students and colleagues of mine. As I looked around, I knew one student on the stage but I knew about 50% of the audience—parents I had in class, grandparents I went to school with. It was 50 years ago that I was inducted into NHS on that very stage. It was a memorable night for me!

Congratulations to the students who are being inducted into NHS tonight and to their family members for their support and caring. (Look at students) You know you didn't get here all on your own. Remember to thank your loved ones.

Scholarship is one of reasons you are here tonight but it's not only scholarship because there are students who receive good grades who are not being inducted. It's the other factors that set you apart – service, leadership and character.

Service is a broad area and for most of you it centers on things you do in your school community or at your church, but in a year or two you'll be leaving Marlington and you need to look at your larger community to continue service. Helping or assisting someone/group or a cause lets you put others and their needs to the forefront instead of focusing on yourself. And doesn't that go against what most people say? You need to look out for Number One! While you do need to take care of yourself, there are so many rewards by helping others. When I retired from Marlington in 2009 after 35 years, I looked for another way to help and serve others. I found Hospice. Hospice is end of life care. It has been one of the most rewarding things I have ever done. Is it sad? Yes, it can be, and yet, I hope that I can comfort their fears about facing death and I marvel at their life stories. Doing a life review is my favorite. Their life stories have been awesome.

It's these types of services that build character and if you listen - really listen, you can learn so much. Character also involves integrity, dependability and being responsible for our own actions. Owning up to our mistakes - and everyone makes them - is a vital part of your character.

According to the dictionary, leadership is both a research area and a practical skill encompassing the ability of an individual or organization to "lead" or guide other individuals, teams, or entire organizations. Have you heard people say, "She or He is a born leader?" They have a magnetic personality and people just gravitate to them. That's not true of all of us. And if it's a practical skill, then it can be learned.

In 1945, Ohio State University conducted a study which investigated observable behaviors portrayed by effective leaders. They were able to narrow their findings to two identifiable distinctions. The first dimension was identified as "Initiating Structure", which described how a leader clearly and accurately communicates with their followers, defines goals, and determines how tasks are performed. These are considered "task oriented" behaviors. The second dimension is "Consideration", which indicates the leader's ability to build an interpersonal relationship with their followers, to establish a form of mutual trust. These are considered "social oriented" behaviors. Each person here is a leader in his/her own way and needs to continue developing his/her own style.

You guys are at a pivotal point in your life. You have the ability to make or break your own life. **Think** about life choices. Oftentimes, you can't control the situation so...It's not what happens to you, it's how you **respond** to what happens to you. That's a key statement. Let me repeat... It's not what happens to you, it's how you **respond** to what happens to you.

When I was young, I remember older people telling me how quickly time flies. I never believed them and now I'm living it. Recently I read an email that hit home for me. So with a few rewrites...

You know time has a way of moving quickly and catching you unaware of the passing years. It seems like yesterday that I was young, and received my NHS pin. Yet in a way, it seems like eons ago, and I wonder where all those years went – most of them at MHS.

I know that I lived them all. I have glimpses of how it was back then and of all my hopes and dreams. But, here it is... I'm in the winter of my life, and it catches me by surprise... How did I get here so fast? Where did the years go and where did my youth go? I remember well seeing older people through the years and thinking that those "older people" were years away from me. I could not fathom it or imagine fully what it would be like.

But, here it is... I'm retired and definitely silver... I move slower and I see an older person when I look in the mirror. Some are in better and some worse shape than me... but, like me, their age is beginning to show and we are now those older folks that we used to see and never thought we'd be.

Now I enter this new season of my life unprepared for all the aches and pains and the loss of strength and ability to go and do things that I wish I had done but never did!! I know that when it's over on this earth... it's over. A new adventure will begin!

Yes, I have regrets. There are things I wish I hadn't done... things I should have done, but indeed, there are also many things I'm happy to have done. It's all in a lifetime.

So, let me remind you, that it will be here faster than you think. So, whatever you would like to accomplish in your life, please do it! Don't put things off too long!! Life goes by quickly. It's never too early to make your bucket list.

LIVE FOR TODAY and say all the things that you want your loved ones to remember.

You too are entering a new season of your life. You are at the beginning of your life story. Make your story full of learning, experiencing new adventures, and follow your dream; you need to at least give your dream a chance so you won't have regrets.

"Life" is a GIFT to you. The way you live your life is your gift to those who come after. Make it a fantastic one.

Again, congratulations.

Special People

To Helen, Our Stepmother
March 1989 – 63rd Birthday

Whatever it is that you want to do,
We have a hat that's just for you.
Be it swimming or sleeping
Or just a walk in the rain,
Cover your head and you won't complain.

If you shower at dusk,
A cap is a must.
If you golf in the sun,
The sun is not fun.
If you sleep on your hair,
Oh no! You don't dare!

So whatever you do on this special day,
All of us just want to say –
Take care of yourself,
Take care of your hair
Because we love you and really do care.

~~~~~~

It's pretty obvious what presents we got Helen for her birthday.

My Aunt Gwen

Even though she's my Dad's sister
She means so much, much more,
Because she was my Mom's best friend,
And what are best friends for?

She introduced my Mom to Dad
And so my story starts
Of how this gentle, uplifting lady
Became a part of our hearts.

I think I'd like to make a list
And probe my memory
Of many things about my Aunt
And what she means to me:

A True Christian
Loving
Disciplined
A tinkling laugh
Singing
Ruffled Doilies
Card Player
Energetic
Values Education
Hard Worker
Sheer white gold star-studded Bed Spread
Well Read
Cookie Maker
A True Friend

These things may not make sense to you.
For me, each tells a story
And in the center is my Aunt

With all her Grace and Glory.

So this year, Aunt Gwen is Ninety
On the seventh day of May.
I hope that she enjoys the fun
And has a Wonderful Birthday!

All My Love,

Written in 2009

~~~~~~

Written for Pam Smith of Atlantic Beach, Florida on September 21, 2009 for her wonderful smile, hospitality and friendship she extended to me during my stay with Linda and her recovery. Pam bought me a coffee cup with mermaids on it and napkins to match since I swam most everyday at her pool. What a nice way to help me remember her warmth and caring attitude.

Pam, You are a comfort giver.
That's just your specialty.
You don't even need to work at it.
For you, it comes naturally.

It's rather chilly here in Ohio.
My mermaid days are done,
But I have such warm memories
Of you, your pool and fun!

My Aunt

How do I say, "I love you"?
How can you possibly feel
All the love I have for you?
It's vibrant, and oh, so real.
Biologically, you're not my Mother,
But you're just as special, you see.
Because you give me love and hope,
You are a "Mother" to me.
You have always been there for me.
Your love it knows no bounds.
I truly thank God every day.
That you have been around.
Your smile fills my heart with joy.
Your guidance keeps me sane.
I look to you for so many things.
At times, I know I'm a pain.
No matter how often I tell you
Words can't express what's in my heart.
Oh, how I love you, my Dear Aunt,
When we're together or when we're apart.

~~~~~

Sandy Harding asked me to write a poem that she could give to
her Aunt. I wrote this for Sandy Stauffenger on October
26, 2010.

Pastor Jonathan Truax

There once was a pastor named Jon
Who had a sweet tooth, 'tis true.
He loved his cookies and ice cream.
He loved his parishioners, too.

One day he went for a long walk
New Baltimore was his destination.
The ice cream store was already closed.
And Jon had to face this revelation.

Now this story has made its rounds
And everyone feels so bad
Because they love their Pastor Jon
And they don't want him sad.

Their love for him grows each year
And they know he likes to dream
So, they thought he could walk the other way
And go get some Handel's ice cream.

~~~~~

Written Oct. 8 for Pastor Appreciation
Read and presented on October 13, 2013
Along with a gift card to Handels

My Uncle Skip

The first words that come to my mind when I think about Uncle Skip are fun-loving, emotional and dedicated.

First of all, let me mention his name Skip. We always thought he was called Skip or Skipper because he was in the Navy. However, when I recently asked him how he got his nickname, he told me since he was the youngest of 10 children that he used to skip to keep up with his siblings – hence they nicknamed him Skip. Actually I was a teenager before I knew his real name was Wendell Eugene.

Here are few gathered tidbits that you may or may not know:

When Skip said he walked two miles to school through all kinds of weather – that's true and that was just to catch the bus for a 10 mile ride to the school.

The old country church where the family attended is called Job's Temple. It still exists and yes, it is on the side of a mountain.

When they were little, Monoca, a niece who is only a couple of years younger than Skip, remembers swimming and splashing with him in the creek that ran by the house and on Sunday afternoons, Gordon (Skip's brother and my dad) and Skip played guitars and sang on the front porch.

Skip was not only ornery and talented - he was smart. He graduated Salutatorian of his high school class.

Karen, my sister, remembers traveling to WV and we met Uncle Skip on the road. We both stopped in the middle of the road to say Hi. Skip said he was on his way to see his girlfriend (Aunt Barb, Now). He was bragging how fast he could make it from his house to hers. He was traveling so fast that you would have thought he was running moonshine and the cops were after him.

One time Karen had a loose tooth so Gordon and Skip tied a string around it and set her on a swing. Gordon held the string and Skip pushed the swing. Uncle Skip snickered the whole time. When Karen got older she figured out that Skip snickered when he was being ornery and having fun.

Like the day Gordon and Skip put running water in Grandma and Grandpa Rinehart's house. When they turned on the water and it worked, Skip took the old tin cups that hung outside by the pump that everyone drank out of and smashed them with a sledgehammer. Grandma was not a happy camper.

I remember going to visit them when they lived in Washington DC. Uncle Skip took us to see the sights. We hopped out of the car and he would pick us up later- just like valet service. While we had fun, Skip basically drove around all day because he said it was easier than finding a place to park.

I started this with saying Skip was fun-loving. Did you ever see Skip when he didn't tell you a funny story or a joke? He usually had a smile on his face and was always ready to laugh.

When Barb & Skip had Marty and Mark the whole family cheered because we finally had some boy cousins to carry on the Rinehart name. Before Marty & Mark, there were 7 girls.

Music was something our family gathered 'round. Most family gatherings included guitars, harmonicas and singing. Carol, another niece, especially remembers those days on the front porch with pickin' and grinnin'. Her favorite song that Uncle Skip did was "Old Shep". Now anyone who has not heard Skip do "Old Shep" has missed a treasure. Carol said when she was around 10 years old; she would look away because she didn't want anyone to see her crying. Well, let me tell you everyone cried when Skip sang that song – including Uncle Skip. And the strange thing was, we always asked him to sing it and we knew everyone was going to cry. At the same time everyone laughed when Skip did his rendition of "The Little Shirt My Mother Made for Me". Music touched his heart and Skip was not afraid to share it. The thing I liked the best was that he never lost the West Virginny twang.

Now Skip lived by a code of ethics. Whether it was his upbringing and/or his years of military training, things fell into black and white categories. He was not bashful about sharing his opinions. And, Heaven help you if you didn't agree. Oh, he mellowed out some as he got older but he was always the gentleman.

He was a dedicated man to God and Country. He got to see a lot of the world during his 21 years in the Navy. He was proud to serve but that came with some sacrifice for Skip and for Barb, Marty and Mark. I came across a song that I thought fit Skip. When I sang it for him a few years back, he choked up but the words speak volumes:

> It's an honor to serve to join in the fight
> To lift up my voice, to lay down my life
> Giving glory to God, seeking none in return
> It's an honor, an honor to serve.

One thing my sister Linda recalls was the love and respect that Skip and Gordon shared. They were truly delighted when they saw each other. Their greeting often went: "Well, hello there brother" "It's good to see you brother" or "How are you doing brother". Over the last several years I had the pleasure of taking Gordon over to visit Skip. They would often reminisce about growing up, their times in the service, or Masonic friends and functions. It was a good life review for both of them and even Aunt Barb and I learned a few things.

I want to end on his dedication to Marty, Mark and most of all, to his wife. He was madly in love and that love continued to grow through the years. They were truly lucky to have so many years together. I can't express it any better than I did at their 60th Anniversary Party.

Sixty beautiful years
have come and passed.
You've proven your bond,
forever shall last.

Sixty beautiful years,
you've been holding hands,
your journey included,
so many plans.

Sixty beautiful years,
memories collected.
During this time,
your souls have connected.

Sixty beautiful years,
you are able to share.
Congratulations, Barb & Skip
we love you and we care.

So last Saturday evening I visualize the family gathering and I hear my Dad saying, "It's good to see you, brother."

Uncle Skip and Dad

MARSHA RINEHART GRAHAM

Weddings and Anniversaries

Dad,   May 1, 1983
I want you to know - I love you.
I want you to feel it too.
I'm so glad that you found Helen,
And happy that she found You.

You know this puts my mind at ease,
And puts my heart to rest -
'Cause Helen will be good for you
And Dad, you deserve the best!

So, during this coming summer
When you take her for your wife,
Be happy; have fun - enjoy it!
Feast on the gifts of life!

In the future when you look back
At the curves life has thrown us,
You'll be glad you made the best
Of all life's precious moments.

Congratulations and
All my love for
Both of you

~~~~~

When Dad announced that he and Helen were getting
married, it was a jolt to my system. I even went into his office
very early one morning and asked him if this was a little fast. I
still chuckle thinking about that, but it had been such a short
time since Mom died and I just wanted him to be sure. He
was. They were. I wrote this poem to reassure them both that I,
too, blessed their relationship.

Happy Anniversary

Twenty-six years ago they say
There was a wedding on Saturday.
It wasn't quite legal if I recall
But I heard the bride was really a doll.

Dot's from Salineville and Gordon's from West 'Ginny.
They scraped every day to save every pinny.
They always dreamt of a beautiful home.
So from West 'Ginny they did roam.

To Alliance, Ohio they did roam.
They found a little house and made it a home.
Two little girls God sent their way,
And now there was another on her way.

Now the Rinehart family was fully grown.
All roots and seed were fully sown.
Gordon and Dorothy's dreams had come true,
And their love had filled their whole lives through.

So, the twenty-first of September
Is a date they'll always remember.
For twenty-six years ago today
Was a very special wedding day.

~~~~~~

Written in September 1972 for my parents' anniversary –

MARSHA RINEHART GRAHAM

Mom lied about her age when she and Dad got married so we always teased them that they were not legally married.

Written for Mom and Dad's 35th and last anniversary in September 1981 - Mom had been fighting cancer for about three years. She passed away about nine months later.

When two people who love each other
Pledge their lives to one another –
The result they say is marital bliss.
Is it true it really happens like this?

Well, thirty-five years ago today,
The wedding bells rang out to say –
Gordon's taken Dorothy to be his wife.
He's pledged to her his love and life.

Now, Dorothy in response to this
Said, "Gordon, I promise you marital bliss.
I'll do my best to be your wife.
You are my love; you are my life."

From that day on and through the years,
They bathed each other's laughs and tears,
The result they say is marital bliss.
I guess it really can happen like this.

Sixty Beautiful Years

Sixty beautiful years
have come and passed.
You've proven your bond,
forever shall last.

Sixty beautiful years,
you've been holding hands,
Your journey included
so many plans.

Sixty beautiful years,
memories collected.
During this time,
your souls have connected.

Sixty beautiful years,
you are able to share.
Congratulations, Barb & Skip
we love you and we care.

~~~~~~

Wendall Eugene Rinehart (Skip), my Dad's brother,
and Barbara Ann (Southall) Rinehart celebrated their
60th Anniversary on September 1, 2015.

About the Author

Marsha Marie (Rinehart) Graham is a retired educator. She earned her Bachelor of Science degree at Kent State University and her Masters from the University of Dayton. During her thirty-five year career at Marlington High School, she taught Biology, Anatomy and Physiology, Spanish I and II, and World Literature. She finished her career as Guidance Director and Dean of Students.

She was raised and still lives in the Marlington School District with her husband of 46 years, Shawn Graham, and their four-legged children. Marsha is very active in her community: Aultman Alliance Hospice Volunteer, Marlington Alumni Association Board of Trustees, Friends of Rodman Library Board, Alliance Music Study Club Executive Board, Aultman Alliance Volunteer Advisory Board, Delta Kappa Gamma, Alliance Area Retired Teachers Association, and Science Hill Community Church.